Finding The Silver Lining In Divorce

What To Do When "I Do" Turns into "I Don't"

Kendra Crowell-Hurd, MA

BALBOA.
PRESS

A DIVISION OF HAY HOUSE

Balboa Press books may be ordered through booksellers or by contacting:

Balboa Press
A Division of Hay House
1663 Liberty Drive
Bloomington, IN 47403
www.balboapress.com
1-(877) 407-4847

Because of the dynamic nature of the Internet, any web addresses or links contained in this book may have changed since publication and may no longer be valid. The views expressed in this work are solely those of the author and do not necessarily reflect the views of the publisher, and the publisher hereby disclaims any responsibility for them.

The author of this book does not dispense medical advice or prescribe the use of any technique as a form of treatment for physical, emotional, or medical problems without the advice of a physician, either directly or indirectly. The intent of the author is only to offer information of a general nature to help you in your quest for emotional and spiritual well-being. In the event you use any of the information in this book for yourself, which is your constitutional right, the author and the publisher assume no responsibility for your actions.

Any people depicted in stock imagery provided by Thinkstock are models, and such images are being used for illustrative purposes only. Certain stock imagery © Thinkstock.

Printed in the United States of America.

ISBN: 978-1-4525-7186-7 (sc)
ISBN: 978-1-4525-7188-1 (hc)
ISBN: 978-1-4525-7187-4 (e)

Library of Congress Control Number: 2013906034

Balboa Press rev. date: 04/23/2013

Also by Kendra Crowell Hurd, MA

Nurture the Garden Within, audiotape, 1996

For my deceased ex-husband, who spoke from heaven, saying "Sign up for your business on the Internet" at the exact time I received a mass e-mail from Balboa Press about self-publishing.

To all the gifted and talented authors who have shared their wisdom with God's people on earth. Thank you for helping me rearrange my molecules.

"In the midst of difficulty lies opportunity."
—Albert Einstein

"Your success and happiness lies in you. Resolve to keep happy, and your joy and you shall form an invincible host against difficulties."
—Helen Keller

"Life is not what it's supposed to be.
It is what it is.
The way you cope with it is what makes the difference."
—Virginia Satir

"I am lovable.
If, earlier in your life, others could not express their love to you, it was because *they* were blocked. Not because of some defect in *you*."
—Dr. Brian Weiss

Table of Contents

Foreword

"The only sadnesses that are dangerous and unhealthy are the ones that we carry around in public in order to drown them out with the noise; like diseases that are treated superficially and foolishly, they just withdraw and after a short interval break out again all the more terribly; and gather inside us and are life, are life that is unlived, rejected, lost, life that we can die of." —Rainer Maria Rilke, *Letters to a Young Poet*

When I first met Kendra Hurd, I was gripped by a fear that I would die with my life unlived, with all my passion and possibility unmet and unexpressed. Working with Kendra and the lessons of this book taught me to live in the *question of a moment*, and for that I am forever grateful. She said, "Know your passion, pursue your passion, and let go of the end," meaning, once you know the seed of your desire, you simply need to water and care for it, and the dream grows itself. I did, and it did—and I never looked back. That day changed my life and put me on a path of living with purpose. I have never regretted one moment since.

Ten years later, when my marriage broke up, I was devastated. But the very day my husband left, a voice in my head spoke, "We're not going off the rails, and you know what to do to stay on track." I never questioned that the "we" in my head was *love*, that which is above and below, available to all of us, all around us, the universe itself reaching out to me. Again, that knowledge was Kendra's gift to me.

I was in the process of editing and producing my first play, a huge undertaking that needed my full focus. I thought, *How am I ever going to do this?* I was so broken by the loss of my marriage.

Looking For The Silver Lining in Divorce: What to Do When "I Do" Turns into "I Don't" was my answer. I took a deep breath, leaned into the lessons that I had learned with Kendra, and two months later, the play went to the stage to sold-out audiences.

The lessons in this book saved my creative soul, the most precious part of me. This book is not just a life preserver; it's the rocket launcher to live inside the awakened spirit, to shine brightly, to step up to the stage of existence with your talent and passion working as partners. You are all that you can believe yourself to be, and this book and its wisdom will deliver you to that place—an authentic life.

If you read any book this year, read this one. Shut off the TV, set your phone aside, and read it two or three times. Only good will come of spending time with these lessons. Practicing these tools will bring the following realization: *there is no one in the world, and I mean no one, I would rather be than me.*

What greater gift could life offer you? Accept the gift, unwrap the possibility, and live to your highest potential.

Amy Sayre Baptista
Master of Fine Arts, Fiction
University of Illinois, Urbana–Champaign
February 25, 2013

The greatest compliment in a mentoring relationship is when the teacher begins learning from the student. Thus has been my twenty-five-year friendship with Kendra Hurd. As I read her book, I heard myself saying, "I believe all these things. I teach these principles." But Kendra writes about them with personal conviction. In seeking understanding and compassion of herself, she has been a role model for her clients and, hopefully, to her colleagues. Kendra's insight is that a teacher's life is but one in a series of stewardships continuing the enlightenment for those following.

Joseph G. Bohlen MD, PhD
Psychiatrist, Associate Professor
SIU School of Medicine
Springfield, IL

Welcome to the conscious portion of your journey. This workbook provides you with a map and many "roads" or "routes" to follow as you journey. As has been stated, there are no right or wrong roads as you journey, only roads and experiences that lead to a more peaceful life. Having experienced and seen firsthand the results of the tools put forth in this workbook, in action and in living color, they work. Kendra has put forth a portion of her journey, and it is no different from that of the rest of us, a journey to wholeness and peace. Her experience is based on trial and error, and this workbook takes some of the guesswork out of the process. All anyone has to do is try, and it is your choice.

These tools will help you become more conscious and aware of your choices and actions. We receive messages every day from the universe, and life is easier when you are aware of them and listen. Blessings and peace to you as you journey.

Bill Crompton,
a grateful friend

Preface

The book that woke me up to the mind/body connection is *Heal Your Body* by Louise Hay. My workbook began fifteen years ago, while I was on a massage table with a sciatic issue. I had returned from a vacation with an old boyfriend, and had come home limping and in pain. Because I had undergone a significant amount of psychotherapy, I knew this previous significant other was not the one for me. However, against my better judgment, I accepted his offer to go on a vacation of my choice (He knew I loved to travel.) While I was on the massage table, the massage therapist asked me, "Do you know what a sciatic issue means in the mind/body connection?" I replied, "What is that?" The massage therapist left the room and returned with the book, *Heal Your Body*. She proceeded to tell me that our spines are about being straight with ourselves, and that I was being hypocritical. That was a *wow* for me, because I knew the book was talking to me. My body was saying what my mouth was not—that, vacation or no vacation, this gentleman was not for me. Since then, *Heal Your Body* has always been correct both for me and for my therapy clients.

One day, while driving home from work, Deb, a friend who is a medium, heard—unsolicited—from my deceased ex-husband. One of the messages he gave her for me was, "Remember to sign up on the Internet for something to do with your business."

(The girlfriend did not know my ex-husband.) The day before, I had received a mass e-mail from Balboa Press about self-publishing. I had been writing this workbook for fifteen years, and wanted to publish: *Looking for the Silver Lining in Divorce: What to Do When "I Do" Turns into "I Don't"* to help other people heal from divorce, or from any other trauma they might have experienced.

I did not pursue this until the following year, when I received another e-mail from Balboa Press after I had asked God to tell me what he wanted me to do with his book—to make it perfectly clear to me, and to help me follow through. Just as I was about to send an e-mail to ask someone to put this workbook on the Internet, I got a phone call and the caller ID said, "Author Services." It was Balboa Press again. This time I listened, and decided to self-publish: *Looking for the Silver Lining in Divorce: What to Do When "I Do" Turns into "I Don't."* My wish is that this workbook will help *empower* you on your spiritual journey to enlightenment, happiness, and healing.

Introduction

After twenty-four years of marriage, the only thing my husband and I agreed on was that he did not like me, and *I* did not like me. Twenty-four years after saying "I do," I said, "I don't." That choice propelled me on a spiritual, healing, mystical journey that continues to enrich my life. Healing after divorce—or any trauma—can be very challenging. The loss of the dream of marriage and family can be devastating, even when you know it is in the best interest of everyone concerned.

Making a decision to make lemonade out of lemons—and to be the best you can be—is a conscious decision. Once that goal has been set, the following "healing tools" can be your guide. Select a healing tool, one at a time, and apply that tool to your everyday life until you feel a pull in your soul to work with another tool. Applying all seventy-one tools can take years. You can practice one tool, ten tools, or more. The investment of time will reap you compound interest with long-term benefits for the rest of your life. These healing tools can help you stay "alive" for the rest of your life (a term coined from the title of Dr. Norman Vincent Peale's book, *STAY ALIVE ALL YOUR LIFE).* While attending therapy during my divorce process, I found a "new love"—therapy! When I started a graduate program (at the age of forty-five), two months after my husband moved out, I had originally signed up for education administration, thinking I wanted to be a principal of a high school (since I had been a business education teacher for ten years). In addition, I signed up for a counseling class. During my teaching career, the high school business education students told me their personal problems, but it took me forty-five years to read the sign on my own forehead that said "Tell me everything you know." After four weeks of my graduate studies, I could hardly force myself to go to the education class, but I could not wait to go to the counseling class. The high school students knew I should be a therapist before I did! At the end of that semester, I changed my major to counseling and was excited to go to class every day. Passion is a heat-seeking missile—it just means that God is the pilot and you are the copilot. An astrological report (by Dana Gerhardt), which I received after I became a therapist, said, I "came here to hold up the Light for other people to See." With an attitude of gratitude, I said thank you to my guides for leading me to my life purpose! My deceased ex-husband had stated through a medium, "Our divorce was a part of the divine plan to help you become stronger." Hearing this, I told myself, *I want to learn my lessons in an easier, healthier way, in my future life times!*

Through a series of mystical and synchronistic experiences, I am self-publishing this workbook. About fifteen years ago, I saw a neon sign in my mind that said "Journey to Wholeness." I wrote it down and then, several nights later, I woke up in the middle of the night and in my journal I wrote thirty-six self-care tools that I felt were dictated to me by God. I have since expanded the number of tools and have had a pull in my soul to publish. About twelve years ago, while she was working on my body, a massage therapist suggested I had a workbook in me. Last year, my deceased ex-husband told a medium to tell me, "Don't forget to sign up on the Internet—something to do with your business." Having just received a mass e-mail from Balboa Press about self-publishing, I signed up. However, I did not follow through with Balboa Press. Doors kept closing in front of me because I was trying to figure out how to publish the book myself. In January 2013, I got another mass e-mail from Balboa Press, and I signed up again. This time I paid attention to the wink from God. On a Monday morning, I said to God, "Let me know what you want me to do with your book—make it perfectly clear, and help me follow through." There were several openings in my counseling schedule (which was unusual) that week, so I figured I would just see what came up. More ideas kept coming to me all week, so I kept writing and adding to my workbook. I was just about to e-mail a webmaster about putting my workbook on the Internet, and the phone rang; my caller ID said "Author Services." It was Virginia from Balboa Press. We had a very easy, flowing conversation. I felt like God was pushing me in the middle of my back. Virginia and I had an appointment to talk on Friday, and I finally decided to practice what I preach. *Walk through open doors. Don't get a stick of dynamite and try to open closed doors. Begin with the end in mind. What do you want to say to yourself when you are ninety?* (This was an exercise I learned at the Mind/Body Medicine continuing-education training at the Harvard Mind/Body Institute in 1996.) *You want to check out of this lifetime with the fewest regrets.* I want to say to myself, *I am glad I tried*, rather than *I wish I had tried*.

You can do it! You can change your life and be happier than you have ever imagined!

The following are mental, emotional, physical, and spiritual tools that I have applied to my life (one tool at a time) since April

1989. I found and continue to find comfort, wisdom, and healing shared by so many gifted, wise authors. I am eternally grateful to these accomplished authors. My wish for the readers of this workbook is that you discover your magnificence! Just begin, one tool at a time!

Chapter 1

Physical Tools:

1. Illness—Find out what your body is trying to say to you. What is your body saying that your mouth is not saying? For example, sinus issues can be complicated by "irritation with someone close—even being irritated with yourself." Before I had ever heard of Mind/Body Medicine, and when I had just become a therapist at the age of forty-eight, I was on a massage table with a sciatic issue. The massage therapist asked me, "Do you know what sciatic issues say in the mind/body connection?" I replied, "What is that?" She replied, "You don't know?" She left the room, returned with *Heal Your Body* by Louise Hay, and gave it to me. According to the book, *sciatic* means, "being hypocritical," not being straight with yourself. (A sciatic issue also relates to "fear of money and the future," according to Louise Hay.) I said, "I think I will hit you when I get off this table." She answered, "My, I must have hit a nerve!" She was correct. I had just returned from a vacation with an old boyfriend that (because of my own therapy process) I knew was not healthy for me. I came home limping and in pain with a sciatic issue! *You Can Heal Your Life* and *Heal Your body by* Louise Hay have never been wrong for me personally, or for any of my clients in my twenty-two years of counseling practice. *All is Well—Heal Your Body with Medicine, Affirmations, and Intuition* by Louise Hay and *Dr. Mona Lisa Schulz* is your guide to wholeness and well -being. My wish is that more medical doctors, health care professionals, and medical schools will discover and utilize the research and wisdom shared in this book.

Notes

2. Exercise—This helps you release stress and stay in shape. Do what your body loves, and you are more likely to continue your exercise or movement program. Exercise. Move your body. If you're inclined, get a personal trainer or a friend to encourage you. (As the title of Dr. Jane Pentz's book asks, *If you don't take care of your body, where else are you going to live?*) It is better to use self-restraint than to deal with feelings of regret.

Notes

3. Eat healthy—Eat fruits and vegetables and more fruits and vegetables. Take a look at *Eat Right 4 Your Type* by Dr. Peter J. D'Adamo. Or try Weight Watchers.

Notes

4. Massage—This helps reduce stress and keeps you out of bed with the wrong people. If you are a touchy/feely person, massage will help you with "skin hunger."

Notes

Chapter 2

Spiritual Tools:

5. Intuition—Listen to your gut; pay attention to synchronicity and coincidences; that's God talking to you. I recommend the following books: *Trust Your Vibes* by Sonia Choquette, *Your Sixth Sense* by Belleruth Naparstek, *The Secret Language of Signs* by Denise Linn, *When God Winks* by Squire Rushnell, *Divine Intuition* by Lynn A. Robinson, and *Second Sight* by Judith Orloff. Coincidence is an accidental sequence of events that appear to have a casual relationship. Sometimes God speaks to us through coincidences. For example, when I was getting a divorce and trying to sell our family home, I looked at a condo on the west side of town. My real estate agent girlfriend said that it was a good deal, on a good street, and that my furniture would fit. (Previously, I had held a Realtor's license and managed commercial property.) I did not really like the condo, but I really liked the woods behind it. Our family home did not sell, and someone else bought the condo. A year went by, and the country home finally sold—and the condo came for sale again at the exact same time. I did not want to live on that side of town, however. I thought I wanted to live on the south side of town where there was a walking path for my big, old Labrador. The Realtor told me that she would not sell me a condo in the south side complex because those condos were not well-built. So I found another real estate agent girlfriend, found a condo I liked on the south side, took a contractor to look at the second condo, and found that the outside bedroom wall had sunk. This was the reason that the master bedroom bed looked like it was going downhill! Needless to say, I went back to the first real estate agent,

looked at the original condo, and decided that God must want me to buy it. Thankfully, I paid attention to the coincidence that the condo had come up for sale again at the exact same time that the family home had sold. Having lived in—and loved—my condo for twenty-two years, I am thankful that I listened to the synchronicity and coincidence. This location is very conducive to my in-home counseling business. God was trying to support me in my future home business that I did not know I was going to have! Coincidentally, I have an astrological report that says I could have a successful home business. My counseling business has been in my home full-time since 2001. *Thank you, God.*

Notes

Notes

6. God of your understanding/church—Put God in the center of your life, and all aspects of your life will work better. (I recommend reading *Feel the Fear and Do It Anyway* by Susan Jeffers.) You can go "church shopping" and notice which church feels good to you. During my divorce process, I visited eight different churches before I found the church I now love. The church that we had been attending as a family did not feel right for me anymore.

Notes

7. Volunteering/giving back—Create a channel to share your gifts. Before our divorce was final in 1991, I was fortunate enough to be involved in helping create a Ronald McDonald House in my hometown. I volunteered eight- to ten-hour days for three years. My therapist said, "You helped build a Ronald McDonald House instead of getting a divorce before your daughter became eighteen." (My husband had moved out one month shy of my daughter's high school graduation and one month shy of her eighteenth birthday.) The therapist said, "Building a Ronald McDonald House to help hundreds of people was a lot healthier than having an affair!" Wow—this was an interesting way to look at my avoidance behavior around what was going on in my own home!

Notes

8. Send blessings—Say, "I am sending blessings," to the one who hurt you. You can ask God to help you mean it. Keep saying it until you mean it. To bless means to expand. Sending blessings to someone is like taking a zipper to heaven; the "good stuff" falls out of heaven on you and the other person. (Thank you to my spiritual director for this tool.)

Notes

9. Spend time in nature—Mother Nature is calming and healing. Get your hands in the dirt (unless you are allergic to dirt or flowers) and plant and nurture a garden. Nature is God's tranquilizer. Help God bring beauty into your life.

Notes

10. Join or start a Mastermind Group—"Where two or three are gathered together and in my name, there am I in the Midst of Them." (Matthew 18:20. Authorized King James Version, The National Bible Press, Philadelphia). Meet weekly or monthly, and pray the same prayer for each person in the group. Then every day, each person prays for the other members of the group. (The resource for establishing a Master Mind Group is from Mastermind Publishing, Warren, Michigan.)

Notes

11. Ask for God's guidance—Ask God to tell you what his will is for you, and then follow and obey. When we are doing God's will for our lives, doors open in front of us. When we don't do God's will, doors close and life is a struggle. Don't get a stick of dynamite and try to open doors that God has closed. Let go and let God. Listen for answers in a dream, gut feelings, intuition, synchronicity, coincidences, number patterns repeating, and/or a repeating pattern of seeing the same animal. I recommend the following books: *Animal-Speak* by Ted Andrews, *Angel Numbers* by Doreen Virtue, *If Christ Were Your Counselor* by Chris Thurman. Here is an example of gut feelings (a knowingness or intuition of God talking to you): for about four months prior to the September 11, 2001, terrorist attacks, I had the feeling that I should go to my stockbroker and have him turn some of my investments into cash. The feeling would not go away, and I could not sleep well. Finally, weeks before 9/11, I went to the stockbroker. He suggested that I might not want to do that. Even though he was the head of the investment firm, I had him do it anyway. After 9/11 he told me that my feelings were very smart and that one other person had done the same thing—a psychologist. Attuned to their intuition, spiritual people are invested in listening to their gut feelings because we know it is God talking to us.

Notes

12. Praying on your knees—Be humble before God. I recommend reading *Praying God's Will for My Life* by Lee Roberts. When the ducks in my pond were getting out of a row and going to different ponds in different states (since everything I was doing wasn't working), I got down on my knees. That is when my life started turning around for the better. My ducks were getting out of a row, so my ducks could get back in a healthier row.

Notes

13. Find what archetype you are living, and if you don't like it, change it—victim, child, warrior, princess, and so on. Read *Sacred Contracts* by Caroline Myss and *King, Warrior, Magician, Lover* by Robert Moore and Douglas Gillette.

Notes

14. Invite your guardian angel to help you—Give your guardian angel a name and ask for help. Angels are just waiting for you to invite them to help you. I recommend the following books and cards to learn more about guardian angels: *Healing with the Angels, Angel Numbers, Messages from your Angels Oracle Cards,* and *Ascended Masters Oracle Cards*—all by Doreen Virtue. I also recommend *Spirit Guides & Angel Guardians* by Richard Webster.

Notes

15. Spirit animal—Ask for a dream to tell you what your spirit animal is. You do not have to go on a vision quest to get your answer. What are the characteristics of that animal? If you are a bear or an eagle, you have few predators; however, if you are a deer, you have numerous predators. Alter your thoughts and behavior so that you are strong and others do not prey upon you. Read *Animal Speak* by Ted Andrews. My spirit animal is a tiger, according to *a dream*. The keynote for a tiger is "Passion, Power, Devotion, and Sensuality." Andrews writes, "When Tiger shows up there will begin to manifest new adventures and renewed devotion and passion for life." That is what has been and continues to manifest in my life. Thank you, tiger, for walking this journey with me!

Notes

16. Pay attention to the animals in your backyard, and to animals that cross your path-- What does that particular animal mean metaphysically? How does that animal apply to you in your everyday life? (*Animal Speak* by Ted Andrews). For example, Native Americans believe that God uses animals to give us messages. In *Animal Speak*, the author lists what different animals mean to the Native Americans. The great blue heron relates to "aggressive self-determination and self-reliance." If the book's explanation of the animal does not make sense to you in the context of your encounter, ask yourself, *What is the animal doing? What is the animal's behavior saying?* In my case, while on vacation in Florida, the blue heron was scanning the ocean, and paying attention to the horizon. The bird was not fishing. It was watching and scanning the ocean's horizon on Anna Maria Island, Florida, where my good friend and I were on vacation. The house we were renting had a deck overlooking the Seven Mile Bridge from Tampa. The first day we were out on the deck, a blue heron was on the gutter of the house next door. He stayed on the gutter for a long time. We took a picture of the bird scanning the horizon—not fishing, just scanning the horizon and the weather. The next day, the bird was back and stayed on the gutter while we were on the deck. The day after that, the blue heron sat on the deck while we looked through a picture window at the bird. It was cool and windy outside, so we did not go out on the deck that day. The day before we were to leave Anna Maria Island, the bird was standing on the deck looking at us through the window—staring us in the eyes. He was not afraid of us and just stared at us through the glass. I knew the bird was trying to tell us something. A few minutes later, we were watching the weather forecast and there was a warning for a heavy storm for that night and the next day. I decided to follow my gut, and my friend agreed—due to my demonstrated conviction that we should leave the island a day early and travel back to Orlando before flying home. As we were leaving the island, we stopped at a beach restaurant to buy T-shirts. We heard a waiter tell the staff that they needed to move the beach party planned for that evening inside, because there was a bad storm coming. After we returned to Illinois, my friend received the security deposit with a note that stated, "You did the right thing by leaving a day early. We had really bad weather after you left—it got very ugly here." The great blue heron was God's messenger about the approaching bad weather because the bird was scanning the horizon for the storm that was coming. There was glass all across the back of our condo, and the ocean was literally two feet off our deck. I can't swim in this lifetime, which added to my anxiety.

Notes

Notes

17. Find out what your aura colors are—What do they mean? If you don't like what they represent, change your thinking and your behavior to heal that particular issue. This is a fun exercise, if you like colors. I recommend reading *What Color Is Your Aura?* by Barbara Bowers.

Notes

18. Embrace change—Change is abundant with possibilities. The Greek philosopher Heraclitus once said, "The only thing constant is change itself." I recommend reading *Embracing Uncertainty* by Susan Jeffers, PhD.

Notes

19. Use astrology to find out what kind of energy you brought to earth-- (Check out www.mooncircles.com by Dana Gerhardt.) One astrology report I read stated that if I were divorced from my husband in this lifetime, it would be the first lifetime with him that I got it right. In other lifetimes, I had stayed. Fortunately, I read that *after* my divorce, so I felt validated. I recommend reading *The Day You Were Born: A Journey to Wholeness through Astrology and Numerology* by Linda Joyce.

Notes

20. Use numerology to find out what your parents "intuitively knew" when they named you-- (Check out www.spiralpath. com by Carol Adrienne.) I was once at a spirituality lecture at our local medical school, and there was an Egyptian man in the audience. He read my name tag and asked if I knew what *Kendra* means in Egyptian. "No," I answered, inquisitively. He informed me that *Kendra* means "center" in Egyptian. I was amazed because "centering" is what I have taught myself to do, and it is part of what I teach the counseling clients God sends me.

Notes

21. Have past life regression therapy to heal any energy leaks from a past life-- Some great books on this subject are *Many Lives, Many Masters, Messages from the Masters*, and *Miracles Happen*—all by Brian Weiss. I have experienced three past life hypnosis sessions, and have seen six different past lives. I was pleasantly surprised after the first session. I saw a *National Geographic* color movie in my mind that I couldn't make up in my wildest dreams! One past life explains why I make a conscious effort to listen to my intuition. In about 1870, I stopped in a town against my gut instinct. I got shot and killed because I was in the wrong place at the wrong time—walking by a bank in a western town when bank robbers were coming out of the bank. In this lifetime, I get anxious when I ignore my gut feelings. Now I know why. Not listening to your gut can sometimes place you in harm's way. Listen to your gut. It is God talking to you. During another past life regression session, I saw myself on a wagon train going from the east to the west with my husband (a man I was in a relationship with in this lifetime for about eight years) and our three children. (One of our children is my cousin in this lifetime, and the other two are friends of mine who were in a relationship together in this life.) When my current life cousin met my significant other (in this life), she put her arms out to hug him—and she is not a touchy-feely person. When my other daughter and husband in that western life met in this lifetime, she said to me, "You need to date him." These two women in this lifetime were saying, "You need to date our father from another life." We indeed go around in soul groups and subconsciously recognize souls from other lifetimes!

Notes

22. Send a prayer request to www.silentunity.org-- The Authorized King James Version of the Bible says, "For where two or three are gathered together in my name, there am I in the Midst of them." (Matthew 18:20).   Type your prayer request, and then at the end type, "Or something better. Thy will be done." God knows what you need. So give God total control to give you what you need.

Notes

23. Find a reputable medium (a person who hears messages from those who have passed over) to help heal any past hurts or unresolved grief-- I recommend reading books by Sylvia Brown, John Edwards, and James Van Praagh. In the fall of 2012, my deceased ex-husband talked to a medium, who then came to my house. My ex-husband talked to her again, and I got to ask questions. Our divorce after twenty-four years was very hurtful, and he was asking for forgiveness. He said the things I had longed to hear while he was alive and we were married. It was a gift from God that was very healing. My deceased ex-husband said that he did not realize the repercussions of his behavior while he was on earth. He continued that he understood things once he experienced his "life review" in heaven. "It is better to process your life issues while on earth rather than waiting to process your issues in heaven," he explained. "Heaven is really all about love!" *Messages from Margaret* by Gerry Gavin will enlighten you one page at a time. This is a must-read if you want to open yourself to spirituality and healing.

Notes

24. Attend a silent retreat-- Take a journal and some good books to read. I flirted with the idea of attending a no-talk ten-day retreat, but instead I started with a one-day retreat and worked my way up to four days. God is in the silence. Now I love silence and enjoy my own company. Become your own best friend. Discover who you are!

Notes

Chapter 3

Mental and Emotional Tools:

25. Taste your words before you spit them out—Stop, take a deep breath, reflect, and choose your words before speaking. Take a meditation class that will help give you a "pause button" for your words. Meditation helps you accumulate healthy chemistry that facilitates having self control when choosing the words you speak.

Notes

26. Cognitive restructuring—Go mining for negative beliefs. (Journaling will help you figure this out faster.) Pinpoint which ideas are not working for you, and then change them. For example, you might have the subconscious belief, *I must be perfect.* Change that belief to *I'm not perfect, but there are parts of me that are excellent.* Another core, subconscious negative belief might be this: *That person got out of bed this morning with the specific goal of ticking me off.* Change that to this belief: *That person did not get out of bed with the specific goal of ticking me off. He got out of bed to go to earth school and learn his lessons—and so did I. Sometimes he bumps into me (and gets grouchy) while he is trying to learn his lessons.* Think instead, *I wonder what happened to him before he got to me today,* or *I wonder what happened to him when he was growing up that caused him to bark at me.* I recommend looking into Mind/Body Medicine training with Dr. Herbert Benson or other practitioners, and reading *Everyday Positive Thinking* by Louise Hay, and *Optimal Thinking* by Rosalene Glickman.

Notes

27. Shadow side—Pay attention to what you say about other people. The parts of ourselves that we deny, we project onto someone else. Own your own shadow side. This concept is truly an eye-opener. I recommend reading *The Dark Side of the Light Chasers* by Debbie Ford. Martha Beck's article "You Spot it, You Got it," in *Oprah's July 2004 Magazine* gives excellent examples of how we humans use projection to deny a part of ourselves.

Notes

28. Sarcasm—Pay attention to sarcastic remarks. Sarcastic remarks are full of hidden anger. Read *The Dance of Anger* by Harriet Lerner. Journaling about the triggers that elicits sarcastic remarks will help you discern where the anger originated.

Notes

29. Finances—The way we deal with money is a metaphor for how we live our lives. Too tight with money = too stingy with our love. Too free with our money = we do not have good boundaries. Balance our checkbook = deal with our life issues. Don't balance our checkbook = don't deal with our life issues. This concept has always been true for me and for my clients, family, and friends. A great book on this topic is *The Energy of Money* by Maria Nemeth.

Notes

30. Chatterbox thoughts—Journal your thoughts and feelings, and discover how your mind jumps from thought to thought. Two wonderful books on the subject are *Women Who Think Too Much* by Susan Nolen-Hoeksema and *Taming Your Gremlin: A Surprisingly Simple Method for Getting Out of Your Own Way* by Rick Carson.

Notes

31. Codependency—Is your happiness dependent on how someone else treats you? If so, own it and find your path to independence and healing. Take the codependency dog collar off and lead *yourself* around. I highly recommend reading *Codependent No More* by Melody Beattie. For three years in a row, I read *The Language of Letting Go*, also by Melody Beattie. Her book is to be read one page a day, to guide us to discern between what we can control and what we can't. After the first year of reading her book, I knew I did not fully understand the control thing, so I actually read it for two more years, one page a day. Control issues are like an economic equation: when feelings of control go up, anxiety goes down. When we feel like we are losing control, anxiety goes up. Once you realize that the only thing you can control is you, you become less anxious and much happier. Once I let go of trying to control other people, I realized controlling myself was a full-time job! For example, I had to control myself to not eat chocolate because I knew it would upset my stomach. Having had two alcoholic grandfathers—both of whom died the year before I was born—set me up for the possibility of alcohol abuse. However, by the grace of God, I don't like alcohol. Instead, I was addicted to sugar. Alcohol is the ultimate sugar high. My parents did not drink, but my mom really liked her chocolate (and her father was an alcoholic).

Notes

32. Stay in the now—Now is the only place where happiness is possible. You cannot have a happier past or present by dwelling on the past. I strongly suggest reading *The Power of Now* by Eckhart Tolle.

Notes

33. Identify and analyze your triggers—Journal to help find out what increases your anger, increases your need to control, and decreases your self-esteem. Then journal and have your therapist help you discover where the repressed anger comes from, and begin the journey to forgiveness and healing.

Notes

34. Love languages—Take a look at these love languages from Gary Chapman: words of affirmation, gifts, physical touch, acts of service, and quality time and conversation. Which of these make you happy? Discover how to love your partner, family, friends, and yourself so that everyone—including you—will feel loved and valued. Read *The 5 Love Languages* by Gary Chapman to learn more about this. Everyone has two primary love languages. When we love ourselves and are loved by others using our two primary love languages, we feel loved. For example, if my two primary love languages are words of affirmation and quality conversation, and I receive a three-carat diamond ring, I am not going to feel loved. The ring is a gift, but I wanted words of affirmation and quality conversation. If you thrive on words of affirmation from others, doing daily positive affirmations can be life changing.

Since 1990, I have been doing daily affirmation work and I will continue for the rest of my life. Affirmations have actually *changed my internal and external world for the better!*

Notes

Chapter 4

Mental, Emotional, and
Spiritual Tools:

35. Journaling—This helps discard negative emotions and helps find love. Emotions are smoke alarms that alert you to look deeper into the "soil of your soul," as suggested by Rev. Dr. Douglas M. Bailey, giving you the opportunity to develop response-ability. In other words, choose your response. Be sure to read *What You Feel You Can Heal* by John Gray.

Notes

36. Therapy—Find a healthier perspective. Raise your self-esteem. Receive validation. Self-esteem is the "immune system of the soul" (Mind/Body Medicine continuing-education training, Harvard Medical School). Therapists are like shoes—they either fit or they don't. Keep looking for the therapist that "fits" for you. Listen to *On Self-Esteem*, an audiotape by Marianne Williamson. When I started therapy two days after my husband moved out in 1989, I wanted to know why I married the person I married. I worked and helped put my husband through college and dental school. He walked out with a doctorate Degree, and I had a bachelor's degree in business education. I could have put myself through a PhD program. Was I angry at myself? That's putting it mildly. One day in therapy, I shared that when I was about twelve and my coal-miner father (whom I adored) was between jobs, he stood on our front porch and told me, "I should have gone to medical school when I returned from World War II." My therapist said, "You put your father through medical school by putting your husband through college and dental school." Fourth of July fireworks went off in my head; I was shocked, but I finally understood and felt enlightened. Since I was a young child, I have been a *why* person.

Notes

37. Affirmations—Say daily affirmations to help reprogram your hard drive (your mind). Affirmations are "fruits and vegetables" for your mind. Whatever we think about *multiplies*. You literally cannot afford the luxury of a negative thought. (Read *You Can't Afford the Luxury of a Negative Thought* by Peter McWilliams.) We tend to get what we expect. So expect the best. Although the origin of the following saying is unclear—it's been attributed to both Mahatma Gandhi and Frank Outlaw—its message *is* clear: "Watch your thoughts, for they become your words. Watch your words, for they become your actions. Watch your actions, for they become your habits. Watch your habits, for they become your character. Watch your character, for it becomes your destiny." I recommend listening to Louise Hay's CD, *Self-Esteem Affirmations*. I also recommend reading *The Self-Talk Solution* by Shad Helmstetter and *Change Your Thoughts, Change Your Life* by Wayne Dyer. A good spiritual affirmation to start with is this: *God and I are partners. I can do all things through God, who strengthens me. I am filled with the life, strength, and energy of God.* (This is from the "daily word" of Silent Unity, a prayer ministry in Unity Village, Missouri.) Another helpful affirmation is this: *I attract all the love, guidance, help, support, and assistance that I need in perfect time and perfect format. I give love, guidance, help, support, and assistance in perfect time and perfect format.* Then give thanks to God when they manifest. Have an attitude of gratitude. Florence Scovel Shinn, in her book, *The Game of Life and How to Play It*, quotes the Bible to substantiate various affirmations.

Notes

38. Visualization—See, in your mind's eye, what you want. What you think about expands, so only see positive present and future situations. Focus on what you want in your life rather than thinking about what you don't have. Your mind is like a satellite dish or radio receiver; you tend to draw to yourself what you think about all day. Make a poster board of pictures of what you want in your life, pictures of you doing what you want to experience in your life. Then see yourself *already* having these situations in your life and *feel* the feelings of happiness and joy. Feelings are the rocket booster to manifestation. For more on the power of visualization, read *Positive Imaging* by Norman Vincent Peale and *The Divine Matrix* by Gregg Braden.

Notes

39. Forgiveness—Buddha said, "Holding on to anger is like grasping a hot coal with the intent of throwing it at someone else—you are the one who gets burned." Forgiveness pulls out the weeds that are choking your healing and growth. Say a "seventy times seven" forgiveness pattern (*thank you to my Spiritual Director*) adapted from Matthew 18:22 in the Bible. For seventy days straight, seven times a day say, "I forgive _____ for any wrongdoings done to me intentionally or otherwise." If you forget one day, you can say it fourteen times the next day. If you forget two days in a row, you have to start the seventy days over. Say it seven times in a row, the same time every day, and mark it off on your calendar. On the seventieth day, say "Amen." Now, here is the challenging part: take about one to two months to make a list of what you appreciate about that person. In order for God to work through us, he wants us to be free of resentment. He wants an open vessel. When I made the list of things that I appreciated about my ex-husband, I came up with ninety-six experiences that I appreciated! That was shocking and healing at the same time. "Seventy times seven" is a spiritual Drano. It flushes out the anger, resentment, and hurt feelings and allows love to enter and remain. I recommend reading *The Blessings of Brokenness* by Charles Stanley.

Notes

40. Ask yourself, *What did I learn from this relationship?*-- Don't lose the lesson. Read *What Smart Women Know* by Steven Carter and Julia Sokol.

Notes

41. Attraction—Ask yourself, *How am I like my former spouse or partner?* I was insulted when my therapist suggested that I was like my ex-husband. After I calmed down, I admitted that I had some work to do on myself. How *were* we alike—mentally, emotionally, physically, spiritually, and sexually? Examine how you were alike with your ex, and if you don't like that comparison, then that is what you can work on healing in yourself so you won't attract the same kind of person next time. Be the kind of person you want to attract. Read *The Secrets of Attraction* by Sandra Anne Taylor, and listen to *The Amazing Development of Men*, a CD by Alison Armstrong.

Notes

42. Divorce support group—Join a divorce support group and learn that you are not the lone ranger.

Notes

43. Dreams—Write your dreams down before you get out of bed, and then analyze what they are trying to tell you. Morning dreams are about finishing processing *asleep* what you did not finish processing while you were *awake*. Dreams in the middle of the night are spiritual dreams, and they have big messages; make sure you write them down. Have a paper and pen beside your bed so you can write down dreams when you awake. When you get out of bed and move your major muscle groups, your subconscious can close and it might be more difficult to recall your dream. *The Mystical, Magical, Marvelous World of Dreams* by Wilda B. Tanner is a wonderful book on the subject. For example, in 1996 I wanted to know if I should pay a sizable amount of money for some postgraduate training at the Mind/Body Medicine Institute at Harvard Medical School. I woke up in the middle of the night because I thought I heard the front door opening. After sitting up in bed, I saw—in my mind's eye—a huge, rounded, walnut door with white mist around it, and I heard a voice say, "This is the door of opportunity ... walk through it." Needless to say, that morning I filled out the application and sent in the deposit. When I attended the training, I did not want to come home because I enjoyed and identified with the research and information presented. The feeling of "finding home" was confirmation that I had attended exactly the right seminar and that I was on a spiritual healing path.

Notes

44. Stay away from married people who want to "date" you-- What they will do *with* you, they will do *to* you.

Notes

45. Hang a "worry basket" in your garage-- before coming into your home or apartment, place your worries in a worry basket, and let God work them out for you.

Notes

46. Neediness—Spend time alone. "If you don't want to spend time alone with yourself, how could you expect another person to want to be alone with you?" (Marianne Williamson, audiotape, *On Self Esteem*) Meditation will help reduce stress chemistry that will eventually help you feel a presence, and that presence feels close, and that presence is God (from Mind/Body Medicine training at Harvard Medical School by Dr. Herbert Benson). Marianne Williamson's audiotape *On Self-Esteem* mentioned earlier, is a great audio tape on this subject. After reading *The Highly Sensitive Person* by Elaine N. Aron, there was a new window into my soul.

Notes

47. Acceptance—What we resist, persists. Say *thank you* to your higher power for the frustrations and *thank you* for the lessons so you do not have to keep repeating the same lessons. This gives the universe the opportunity to give you your highest good, and allows you to move on to a higher lesson.

Notes

48. Gratitude—Gratitude is the currency of angels. Zig Ziglar said, "The more you recognize and express gratitude for the things you have, the more things you will have to express gratitude for." Get a journal and dedicate it to gratitude. Make a daily list of things you are grateful for, and experience your life getting easier. For more on this subject, read *Attitudes of Gratitude* by M. J. Ryan.

Notes

49. Ego—"Edging God out. There are two feelings in the world—fear and love. Fear is an absence of Love. Love is the presence of God" (*A Course in Miracles* by Helen Schucman).

Notes

50. Consider joining a *Course in Miracles* study group-- Have the intention of leading from your higher self—every day before you get out of bed, have this intention. Before getting out of bed, say, "God, thank you for being with me today: above me, below me, beside me, in front of me, behind me, underneath me, and inside of me." If you forget to say that, get back in bed and say this prayer, and then get up and get ready for the day. My goal is for God to be the pilot in my life, and I am the copilot—listening to God's loving guidance for my highest good.

Notes

51. Let go of guilt and shame—They lower your energy vibration. Forgive yourself and others. Forgiveness raises your energy vibration. Two great books about this are *Guilt Is the Teacher, Love Is the* Lesson by Joan Borysenko and *Healing the Shame That Binds You* by John Bradshaw.

Notes

52. Walk a medicine wheel—Native American culture teaches us to walk the medicine wheel with a question in mind. (Sedona, Arizona, is a spiritual energy place that is magical for walking a medicine wheel.)

Notes

53. Find music that soothes your soul-- Playing a musical instrument can be healing for the soul. An interesting book on the powerful effects of music is *The Mozart Effect* by Don Campbell.

Notes

54. Be what you want to attract—make a list of what you want in a partner and then ask yourself, *Am I that person?* If you are not that person, this is what you need to work on. If you want "the fruit of the Spirit" (Galatians 5:22) in a partner— "love, joy, peace, patience, kindness, goodness, faithfulness, gentleness, and self-control" (Galatians 5:22–5:23)—then in order to attract that kind of person, you need to *be* that kind of person. I don't know about you, but I realized I had some work to do on myself!

Notes

55. Increase self-esteem—Self-esteem is what you think of yourself. "Other-esteem" is what other people think of you. (Read *What You Think of Me Is None of My Business* by Terry Cole-Whittaker.) Treat yourself like your own best friend. Two great books to read are *Simple Abundance* by Sarah Ban Breathnach and *The Art of Extreme Self-Care* by Cheryl Richardson.

Notes

Chapter 5

Mental, Emotional, Physical,
and Spiritual Tools:

56. Have energy medicine treatments: Reiki, Healing Touch, or Therapeutic Touch treatments—God's energy is channeled to raise your energy vibration to improve your own natural immune system. Reiki is a spiritual healing art, the practice of transmitting healing energy through the hands (like laying on of hands from the Bible). This universal energy supports the body's inherent self-healing abilities. You lie on a massage table or recline in a chair, fully clothed. For me personally, as well as for God's clients that he sends to me, energy medicine is a game changer. It helps you heal the crust around your heart from emotions like anger, resentment, rejection, abandonment, and grief. I encourage you to read *Hands of Light* by Barbara Ann Brennan and *The 7 Healing* Chakras by Brenda Davies. "The Reiki method is not only for curing illness. Its true purpose is to correct the heart-mind, keep the body fit, and lead a happy life using the spiritual capabilities human beings were endowed with since birth" (Mikao Usui, who developed the Reiki method). (*Thank you to several dear nuns and other healing practionners.*) In 2012, while I was receiving a Reiki treatment, the Reiki practitioner saw Jesus on one side of me, and an angel holding a tray on the other side of me. Jesus said to her, "Get the black rope out of her abdomen. Pull it out. It must come out." The Reiki healer visually pulled a black rope out and laid it on the angel's tray. For years, I had been having gastrointestinal issues and could not figure out why. What came up for me when I went home that day was that in a past life in about 1430, I was married to an abusive alcoholic; we had four children, and I had an affair. The alcoholic husband of that lifetime found out and burned the house down. He had tied me up with a rope, and that is why my kids and I did not get out of the burning house. Energetically, I had brought the energy of that lifetime with me into this one. Amazingly, I felt relief that I had not known for years! Thank you, Jesus!

Notes

Notes

57. Practice chanting and/or drumming—It releases negative energy and raises your energy vibration.

Notes

58. Practice feng shui in your home, office, and garden—This ancient practice will help draw positive energy to you. De-cluttering is a good way to start. When my feng shui consultant walked into my condo for the first time, she said, "You have too much stuff in here." It took me almost a year to de clutter each drawer, closet, every cabinet, the garage, and the basement. Now I like my condo so much more. She told me, "Energy is female, and she likes to meander. If you have clutter on the floor, the energy gets stuck and is stagnant." Now, if I purchase something new at our local art fair, I rotate my favorite knickknacks! It also cuts down on spending! I recommend Lillian Too's books about feng shui: *Total Feng Shui* and *The Complete Guide to Feng Shui.*

Notes

59. Live a balanced life—In a month's time, spread your energy in the following areas: "higher power, career, relationship, family, friends, hobby, leisure, contribution, and self-awareness." (From *Feel the Fear and Do it Anyway* by Susan Jeffers.) Remember a relationship is one-ninth of a balanced life. Estrogen is famous for putting more energy into a relationship and letting the other areas suffer. I suggest reading *Feel the Fear and Do It Anyway* by Susan Jeffers.

Notes

60. Practice the relaxation response and meditation—"The essence of silence is joy and bliss" (adapted from *The Perfect Sage*— Hindu text meaning finding joy ever within himself). Just think of meditation as "mental floss" (Frank and Ernest). "The best cure for the body is a quiet mind," said Napoleon Bonaparte. Take deep diaphragmatic breaths, and clear your mind. Practice three to four times a week, for ten to twenty minutes each time. When I started meditating, I could not sit still for three minutes. If you're interested, take a meditation class. It took me nine months of practice to be able to sit still for thirty minutes and meditate. "Be still, and know that I am God" (Psalm 46:10). Some helpful books include *Meditations to Heal Your Life* by Louise Hay, *The Relaxation Response* by Herbert Benson, and *Meditations for Manifesting* by Wayne Dyer.

Notes

61. Spend time with a hobby you enjoy—What did you enjoy as a child? Buy some toys that you played with as a child, and heal the child within. I recommend a book titled the same: *Healing the Child Within* by Charles L. Whitfield.

Notes

62. Take a vacation—Getting out of town helps you gain a different perspective. Taking a vacation from electronic devices can also be helpful!

Notes

63. Recognize your stress warning signals, and change what you are doing to get a different result—Recognize your physical, emotional, mental, behavioral, and spiritual warning signals. Some of these are headaches, indigestion, tight neck and shoulders, bossiness, grinding of teeth, inability to get things done, crying, anxiety, boredom, anger, loneliness, getting upset easily, forgetfulness, constant worry, excessive/compulsive thoughts, emptiness, lack of purpose, shame, fearfulness, and powerlessness. These warning signals are from Mind/Body Medicine research from the Harvard Medical School.

Notes

64. New relationship—It can be advantageous to spend time with people to get to know them before you make a commitment. Find out if they follow through on their word. Are they honest and trustworthy? Are you compatible? It can take three to six months to find out. Then it takes a minimum of eighteen to twenty-four months to find out what a person is truly like. You want to see that person in all four seasons twice before you move in or marry. The Bible says in Galatians 5:22, "The fruit of the Spirit is love, joy, peace, patience, kindness, goodness, faithfulness, gentleness, and self-control." The following are some wonderful books about relationships: *Are You the One for Me?* by Barbara De Angelis, *Love Is Letting Go of Fear* by Gerald Jampolsky, *Redefining Mr. Right* by Janet Giler and Kathleen Neumeyer, *What's Love Got to Do with It?* by Nancy Pollard, and *When God Winks on Love* by Squire Rushnell.

Notes

65. Clear out the clutter in your home—Release the old and make way for the new. Decluttering can be challenging. Getting the job done is tied to emotional issues that we have not yet released. Many times over the years, I have gone to a closet or a drawer with the intention of cleaning out that space, yet I found myself thinking *not today.* Eventually, I grew to understand that I was still holding on to some emotional baggage. You have more learning opportunities to *let go* of old emotional baggage so you can clear out your physical space. It is time well spent. Now I like myself— and my living space— much more! I actually have more room to breathe inside of me and in my surroundings. When you donate your used items, say *thank you* to them for serving you, and make a wish that they will enhance someone else's life. *Space Clearing* by Denise Linn is recommended reading for this topic.

Notes

66. Menopause—It is a time when our chemistry asks, "When is it my turn?" A terrific resource for this time in a woman's life is *The Wisdom of Menopause* by Christiane Northrup.

Notes

67. Emotional eating—Journal to discover what is eating you. I recommend the following two books for more on emotional eating: *You Can't Quit 'til You Know What's Eating You* by Donna LeBlanc and *When Food Is Love* by Geneen Roth.

Notes

68. Burn sage or a green candle to clear any negative energy in your home and office-- Walk around each room and say, "I am releasing any negative energy in this room and replacing it with positive, loving energy."

Notes

69. Clear jewelry with a sage candle, or place it outside for twenty-four hours, and say, "I am releasing any negative energy in this piece and leaving only positive, loving energy." (This idea is from a workshop with Dr. Brian Weiss in Denver, Co in the early 1990s.)

Notes

Do Something:

70. Create your own path to health and happiness from the suggested laundry list-- You could start with *Everyday Positive Thinking* by Louise Hay. Go to church. Go to school. Take a class. Exercise. Play a musical instrument and/or sing. Get a degree. Draw, paint, sing, dance, study a foreign language, or travel. Meditate. Read a book. Write a book. Have a feng shui consultant help you raise the energy vibration in your home. Have a Reiki, Healing Touch, or Therapeutic Touch treatment, and raise your energy vibration (this is a game changer). Just *begin*. "If you always do what you have always done, you will always get what you always got" (*Excuses Begone!* by Wayne Dyer).

Notes

71. Pray this simple prayer-- *I am sending love and blessings from my higher self to _____'s higher self.* (Higher self represents our God center.) It is like sending a spiritual e-mail to another person. It helps soften the other person, as well as yourself. The prayer opens the heart centers of both individuals.

"The most satisfying journey you will ever undertake—and a mark of an enlightened human being—is to discover how to build a sense of happiness that no one can take away from ..." (Deepak Chopra).

"Remember that you are lovable. If, earlier in your life, others could not express their love to you, it was because they were blocked, not because of some defect in you" (*Healing the Mind and Spirit* cards, Brian Weiss).

My wish is that you find comfort in the wisdom expressed by all these gifted and talented authors who have shared their healing tools in their books, CDs, and cards. I wish you the best on your journey to a healthier and happier life. I am forever grateful for the healing and happiness I have received by reading, studying, and applying these wonderful tools. These authors have many more books than are mentioned in this workbook, all of which have added to my enlightenment, peace, and happiness. If you see a title that interests you, buy that book—there will be something in it that will speak to you.

"Today is the first day of the rest of your life" (Anonymous). Best wishes in nurturing your garden within and becoming the best you can be!

Notes

Notes

Acknowledgments

If anyone had told me I would write a book, I would have thought, *Who, me?* This book has been rolling around in my head and on paper for about fifteen years. I finally decided, with a little push from heaven, to give it a try. After experiencing a challenging marriage and divorce, I thought many times, *There must be a better way to emotionally walk on hot coals with shoes on instead of emotionally getting your feet burned every day.* My wish is to help other people by giving them a list of tools to use as road maps for their healing journeys.

There are so many people who have been angels and cheerleaders for me during my life. I hope I can name them all. First, I want to thank my Italian grandparents for crossing the vast ocean and coming to the United States at the ages of eighteen (Grandpa Pete) and thirteen (Grandma Marianne). Unable to speak English and without any schooling, they forged their path and settled in southern Illinois. Fortunately, my parents lived next door to them, and we always had fresh fruits and vegetables and chicken. After much begging on my part, my parents, Kenneth and Margaret, allowed me to go to college five hours away from home rather than forty-five minutes from where we lived.

My father was a coal miner for twenty-five years. After he

went to heaven, I took a tour of a previously active coal mine, and I gained new respect for my father; he had worked underground, bent over, with a canary in a bird cage to let the coal miners know if it was safe that day underground. My parents gave me a huge jump-start in life by paying for me to attend college and to become a high school teacher. Teaching high school business education gave me a lot of experience with students from varying backgrounds, all of whom I treasured and enjoyed.

My beautiful daughter, Tracy, and her husband, Mike, have gifted me with three wonderful, talented, God-loving grandchildren, Alli, Gavin, and Teagan. When Tracy was young, she loved horses. I was afraid of horses, and I only interacted with them while I was standing on the ground. After taking Tracy to tap, ballet, tumbling, and piano lessons, I finally let go of my fear of horses and allowed her to follow her passion of dressage, stadium, and cross-country jumping. Because Tracy loves horses, she taught me how to brush, feed, and clean horse stalls—something I would never have experienced if not for her. Thank you, God, for giving my ex-husband and I such a wonderful daughter. Thank you, Tracy, for all the fun memories. Our children come into their lifetimes with us with something already on their hard drives. We, as parents, get to write on their hard drives, but God has already written other programs onto their hard drives. I am thankful I honored her internal hard drive from God and supported her in her dream of riding horses.

God has blessed me with so many loving and entertaining family members and friends who had my back—when I couldn't find my back. I am eternally grateful to JoLynn, Donna and Tom, Carol, Marilyn and Wayne, Aunt Elda and Uncle Tom, Bonnie,

Chick and Pat, Denise, Marion, Deb, Sandy, Cathy, Mary Kay, Sharon, Andrea, Linda and Bill. Thank you for being there for me when I needed you. Thank you to my cousin Schy, who held my hand while I learned how to turn on and use my new Apple computer. Thank you, one and all. I know many angels are watching over all of you.

Earth angels do exist, and I have been graced with the friendship of three special nuns: Sister Ann, Marie Claire, and Melanie—as well as numerous energy practitioners. Thank you for sharing your friendship and your gift of energy medicine. Energy medicine helps me release the crust around my heart from my divorce. Thank you to God's earth angels.

The year I was pregnant with our daughter, my ex-husband shared that he wanted to go to college and become a history teacher. (I was a business teacher at the time, and he was a dental technician.) When my ex-husband and I were twenty-eight years old and our daughter was two, he started dental school. I taught business education in St. Louis County, Missouri, while he was attending dental school. Mildred was the head of the business department in St. Louis where I worked. She was incredible to work for, and I feel honored to have worked with her. When my ex-husband graduated and we moved back to Springfield, Mildred and I stayed friends. Eighteen years later, during our divorce and while I was working on my master's degree, Mildred graciously invited me to live with her for free; I did not have a job, and I was doing an internship at an adolescent psychology unit in St. Louis County. She re-parented me during those months of living with her. I know heaven opened the gates wide for her when she crossed over. She was another one of my earth angels.

Thank you, Mildred. I will always remember you with love and gratitude.

Thank you to Dr. Joe and Dr. Terry, who gave me my first therapist job when I was forty-eight years old. They owned an adolescent boys' home, and working there gave me X-ray vision into adults. After reading the boys' files and doing therapy with them for five years, I grew to understand why we all do the things we do. They taught me invaluable lessons that cannot be learned by reading a book or attending a lecture.

The Mind/Body Medicine continuing-education training from Harvard Medical School gave me so much confidence. Their research backed up all the books I had been reading and applying to my life and using with my counseling clients. I came home from that training with renewed vim, vigor, and vitality. Thank you, Dr. Herbert Benson and colleagues.

God has blessed me with so many wonderful clients over the years. I treasure watching them blossom! Thank you for trusting me enough to share your stories with me. I feel honored.

Thank you to my ex-husband, who propelled me on an empowerment journey; I don't know how I would have found this path without our divorce. He said from heaven that our difficult marriage and divorce was a contract that we made before we were incarnated so that I could become strong. When we were young, he called me "Misty." His soul knew my soul was mystical before I knew I was mystical. Thank you, Bob.

Two loving and wonderful men have been in my life since the divorce. They each taught me to love again. Thank you, Larry and Bill. Your kindness, consideration, and gentle love taught me there is another way to live—with happiness. Bless you both on your own journeys.

Virginia from Balboa Press called me the very morning that I had asked God to let me know what he wanted me to do with his book, making it perfectly clear to me and helping me follow through. She had perfect timing. The phone rang, and the caller ID said, "Author Services." Thank you, Virginia, for your perfect timing. Stephanie from Balboa Press has been so patient and kind and helpful. This workbook would not have been possible without all the angel guides from Balboa Press—Andrea, Tiffany, and Fatima. Thank you to one and all.

Without all the gifted authors whom I have read and continue to read, this healing, mystical, magical, spiritual journey would not have been possible. These authors, and others not mentioned, have shared their gifts with the world through the written word and have forever changed—and continue to change—people's lives … including mine. And, most of all, "Thank you to God!"

Thank you, and God bless.

Bibliography and Suggested Reading

Andrews, Ted. *Animal Speak.* St. Paul: Llewellyn Publications, 2004.

Armstrong, Alison. *Amazing Development of Men.* Audio presentation on compact disc. Sherman Oaks, CA, Pax Programs, Inc., 2005

Aron, Elaine. *The Highly Sensitive Person, NY,* Carol Publications, *1996.*

Beattie, Melody. *Codependent No More.* Center City,*MN,* Hazelden Publishers, *1986.*

_____. *The Language of Letting Go,* Center City, Hazelden Publications, *1990.*

Beck, Martha. *Oprah Magazine,* "You Spot It, You Got It," July 2004.

Benson, Herbert. *The Relaxation Response, NY,* Harper Collins Publishers, *2000.*

Borysenko, Joan. *Guilt Is the Teacher, Love Is the Lesson,* NY, Time Warner, 1991 .

Bowers, Barbara. *What Color Is Your Aura? NY,* Pocket Books, *1989*

Braden, Gregg. *The Divine Matrix, USA,* Hay House, Publishers, *2007.*

Bradshaw, John. *Healing the Shame That Binds You,* Deerfield Beach, FL, Health Communications, Inc., 1993

Breathnach, Sarah Ban. *Simple Abundance.* NY, Warner Books, *1995.*

Brennan, Barbara Ann. *Hands of Light.* NY, Bantam Books, 1987.

Campbell, Don. *The Mozart Effect.* Harper Collins Publishers, 2001.

Carson, Rick. *Taming Your Gremlin: A Surprisingly Simple Method for Getting Out of Your Own Way.* NY, Harper Collins Publishers, 2003.

Carter, Steven, and Julia Sokol. *What Smart Women Know.* NY, Dell Publications, 1990.

Chapman, Gary. *Five Love Languages.* Chicago, Northfield Publishers, *1992.*

Choquette, Sonia. *Trust Your Vibes.* Carsbad, CA, Hay House Publishers, 2004.

Cole-Whittaker, Terry. *What You Think of Me Is None of My Business.* Penquin Group, 1988.

D'Adamo, Peter J. *Eat Right 4 Your Type*. NY, G. P. Putnams & Sons Publisher, 1996.

Davies, Brenda, M.D. *The 7 Healing Chakras*. Berkeley, CA, Ulysses Press, 2000.

De Angelis, Barbara. *Are You the One for Me?* NY, Dell Publishing, *1992*.

Dyer, Wayne. *Change Your Thoughts, Change Your Life*. USA, Hay House Publishing, 2008.

_____. *Excuses Begone!* USA, Hay House Publishing, 2011.

_____. *Meditations for Manifesting*. Audiobook. USA, Hay House Publishing, 1995.

Ford, Debbie. *Dark Side of the Light Chasers*. NY, Penquin Group, 2010.

Gavin, Gerry. *Messages from Margaret*. USA, Hay House Publishing, 2012.

Giler, Janet, and Kathleen Neumeyer. *Redefining Mr. Right*. New Harbinger Publishers, 1992.

Glickman, Rosalene. *Optimal Thinking*. Wiley, John & Sons, Inc. 2002.

Gray, John. *What You Feel, You Can Heal*. NY, Harper Collins Publishers, 2005.

Hay, Louise. *Everyday Positive Thinking.*USA, Hay House Publishers, 2004.

_____. *Heal Your Body*. Carson, CA, Hay House Publishers, 1982.

_____. *Meditations to Heal Your Life*. Carlsbad, CA and NY, Hay House Publishers, 2000.

_____. Self-Esteem Affirmations. Audio CD. USA, Hay House Publishers, 1990.

_____. *You Can Heal Your Life*. Carlsbad, CA, Hay House, Inc. 1999.

Hay, Louise and Schulz, Mona Lisa. *All is Well with Medicine, Affirmations, and Intuition*. USA, Hay House, Inc., 2013.

Helmstetter, Shad. *Self-Talk Solution*. Pocket Books, 1988.

Jampolsky, Gerald. *Love Is Letting Go of Fear*. NY, Random House, 1979.

Jeffers, Susan. *Embracing Uncertainty*. NY, St. Martin's Press, 2003.

_____. *Feel the Fear and Do It Anyway*. NY, Ballantine Books, 1987.

Joyce, Linda. *The Day You Were Born: A Journey to Wholeness through Astrology and Numerology*. NY, Kensington Publishing, 1998.

LeBlanc, Donna. *You Can't Quit 'til You Know What's Eating You*. Deerfield Beach, FL, Health Communications, 1990.

Lerner, Harriet. *The Dance of Anger*. NY, Harper & Row Publishers, 1985.

Linn, Denise. *The Secret Language of Signs*. NY, Ballantine Books, 1996.

_____. *Space Clearing*. US, Hay House Publishers, 2001.

McWilliams, Peter. *You Can't Afford the Luxury of a Negative Thought*. Los Angeles, Prelude Press, 1988.

Moore, Robert, and Douglas Gillette. *King, Warrior, Magician, Lover*. NY, Harper One, 1991.

Myss, Caroline. *Sacred Contracts*. NY, Harmony Books, 2001.

Naparstek, Belleruth. *Your Sixth Sense*. NY, Harper Collins Books, 1997.

Nemeth, Maria. *The Energy of Money*. NY, Ballantine Publishing Group, 1997.

Nolen-Hoeksema, Susan. *Women Who Think Too Much*. NY, Holt, Henry & Co., 2004.

Northrup, Christiane. *The Wisdom of Menopause*. NY, Bantam Books, 2001.

Orloff, Judith. *Second Sight*. NY, Warner Books, 1996.

Peale, Norman Vincent. *How to Make Positive Imaging Work for You*. NY, Foundation for Christian Living, 1982.

_____. *Stay Alive All Your Life*. New York, Prentice-Hall, Inc. 1957.

Pentz, Jane Dr. *If You Don't Take Care of Your Body, Where Else Are You Going to Live?* Lifestyle Management Associates, 2010.

Pollard, Nancy. *What's Love Got to Do with It?* Park City, Utah, Benchmark Publishers, 1993.

Richardson, Cheryl. *The Art of Extreme Self-Care*. USA, Hay House Publishers, 2009.

Roberts, Lee. *Praying God's Will for My Life*. Nashville, TN, Nelson, Thomas Inc., 2002.

Robinson, Lynn A. *Divine Intuition. NY, Dorling* Kindersley Publishing, Inc., *2001.*

Roth, Geneen. *When Food Is Love*. NY, Plume/Penguin Group, 1992.

Rushnell, Squire. *When God Winks*. NY, Atria Books, 2001.

_____. *When God Winks on Love*. NY, Atria Books, 2007.

Ryan, M. J. *Attitudes of Gratitude*. San Francisco, CA, Conar Press, 1999.

Schucman, Helen. *A Course in Miracles. Glen Ellen CA,* Foundation for Inner Peace, 1975.

Scovel Shinn, Florence. *The Game of Life And How to Play It*. Camarillo, CA, DeVorss Publications, 1925.

Stanley, Charles. *The Blessings of Brokenness*. Grand Rapids, MI, Zondervan, 1997.

Tanner, Wilda B. *The Mystical, Magical, Marvelous World of Dreams*. Tahlequah, OK, Sparrow Hawk Press, 1988.

Taylor, Sandra Anne. *The Secrets of Attraction*. USA, Hay House Inc., 2001.

Thurman, Chris. *If Christ Were Your Counselor.* Nashville, TN, Thomas Nelson Publishers, *1993.*

Tolle, Eckhart. *The Power of Now. Novato, CA, New World Library, 2004.*

Too, Lillian. *The Complete Guide to Feng Shui. NY, Barnes & Noble, Inc., 1996.*

_____. *Total Feng Shui.* San Francisco, Chronicle Books, *2005.*

Virtue, Doreen and Brown, Lynnette. *Angel Numbers.* USA, Hay House Inc., *2005.*

Virtue, Doreen. *Ascended Masters Oracle* Cards. USA, Hay House, 2007.

_____. *Healing with the Angels.* Carlsbad, CA, Hay House, Inc., 1999.

_____. *Messages from Your Angels Oracle Cards.* Carlsbad, CA, Hay House, *2002.*

Webster, Rickard. Spirit Guides & Guardian Angels. St. Paul, MN, Llewellyn Publishers, *2002.*

Weiss, Brian. *Healing the Mind and Spirit Cards.* Carlsbad, CA, Hay House, 2003.

_____. *Many Lives, Many Masters.* NY, Simon & Schuster, *Inc., 1988.*

_____. *Messages from the Masters.* NY, Warner Books, Inc., *2000.*

_____. *Miracles Happen.* NY, Harper Collins Books, *2012.*

Whitfield, Charles. *Healing the Child Within.* Deerfield Beach, FL, Health Communications, Inc., 1987.

Williamson, Marianne. *On Self-Esteem.* Audiocassette, Harper Audio Lecture, 1992.

Other References/ Suggested Sources

Books by Sylvia Brown, John Edwards, and James Von Praaagh.

Daily Word, Silent Unity, Unity Village, Missouri.

Mastermind Publishing. Warren, Michigan.

Matthew 18:20. Authorized King James Version, Philadelphia, The National Bible Press.

Mind/Body Medicine continuing-education training with Dr. Herbert Benson at Harvard Medical School.

www.mooncircles.com.

www.spiralpath.com.

www.silentunityprayerrequest.

About the Author

Kendra Hurd is a Licensed Clinical Professional Counselor and a National Certified Counselor in private practice in Springfield, Illinois. She has a master's degree in Human Development Counseling from the University of Illinois–Springfield, and a bachelor's degree in business education from Western Illinois University. Ms. Hurd is certified by Harvard Medical School's clinical training program in Mind/Body Medicine—a recognized field of medical research and practice that studies the effects of stress on the human body. She became a therapist in 1991 after investing time and energy in divorce therapy because of the breakup of her twenty-four-year marriage. She found a new "love"—therapy.

Ms. Hurd was involved in the founding of the Ronald McDonald House in Springfield, Illinois, in 1985. She was also on the steering committee to establish a Festival of Trees in Springfield in 1990. Ms. Hurd has given talks on stress hardiness in the central Illinois area, in San Diego, and at the American Community School in Cobham, England (now known as ACS International Schools). Kendra is certified in Reiki Level II and Healing Touch Level I training.

24890977R00120

Made in the USA
Lexington, KY
04 August 2013